Wei's Part-Time Job

I Talk You Talk Press

CONTENTS

CHAPTER ONE

Wei Liu is from Beijing, China. He is studying English at a college in New York. He loves studying English, and he loves living in New York. But it is expensive. He needs money. So, he has a part-time job. He has no lessons at college on Friday mornings, or on Saturdays and Sundays. So he works at a hotel on Friday mornings, Saturday mornings and afternoons, and Sunday mornings and afternoons. In the morning, he cleans the hotel rooms. In the afternoon, he helps on the front desk.

The hotel is small and cheap. It has a manager and ten workers. Wei likes his manager and his co-workers. Everyone is very kind.

It is Friday morning. Wei arrives at the hotel at 9:00am. One of his co-workers, Sandra, is in the staff room. Sandra is 50. She likes Wei very much. She helps him with his job, and with his English.

"Good morning, Wei. How are you today?" says Sandra.

"I'm nervous," says Wei.

"Nervous? Why?" asks Sandra.

"Because I have an important English test this afternoon. I want to study this morning, but I have to work."

Sandra smiles. "Did you study last night?"

"Yes, I did," says Wei. "I studied until two am this morning!"

"Two am? That's late! Are you tired?" asks Sandra.

"Yes, I am," says Wei. "Working and studying is hard. But I need the money."

"I understand," says Sandra. "My son is a student. He has a job, too. Students need money. Good luck in your test this afternoon. Let's start work. I am going to clean the rooms on floors two and three. You are going to clean the rooms on floors four and five."

"OK," says Wei. He puts on his work jacket. "Let's start."

They walk out of the staff room and go to the cleaning room. They pick up clean sheets, clean towels and cleaning items. Wei puts everything on his cart and walks to the staff elevator. He goes up to floor five.

I'm going to work quickly today, he thinks. *My test starts at three pm. I want to study a little before the test.*

Wei gets out of the elevator. He knocks on the first door, and opens it. He goes into the room.

Sometimes the rooms are very clean. Sometimes, they are very dirty. This room is dirty. He cleans the bathroom and changes the sheets on the bed.

I don't like this job, he thinks. *I don't like cleaning toilets and changing sheets. But, I need the money.*

He goes to the next room. This room is cleaner. He cleans the bathroom and changes the sheets quickly. He goes to the next room, and then the next. When he finishes the 5th floor, he takes the elevator down to the 4th floor.

He looks at the time. I finished the fifth floor quickly, he thinks. *If I finish the fourth floor quickly, maybe I can finish work early. I will ask the manager.*

CHAPTER TWO

Wei opens the door to room 401. It is very clean. He is happy.

He cleans the bathroom and puts new towels on the towel rack. He puts the used towels on his cart. Then, he changes the sheets. After that, he looks at the table. There is a glass of water on the table. Wei cleans everything carefully. He uses a cloth to clean the table. But he is thinking about his test. He knocks over the glass of water.

Oh no! he thinks. *The tissues!* The water goes into the tissue box. The tissues are very wet.

Wei takes out the wet tissues. Then, he feels something.

There is something inside the tissue box, he thinks. *There is something hard. It feels cold. What is it?*

He pulls the item out.

It is a necklace! he thinks. *A diamond necklace! Why is it here, in the tissue box in this hotel room?*

He looks at the necklace.

This is expensive, he thinks. *Is it the guest's necklace?*

He looks around the hotel room. There are no bags. There is no suitcase. Usually, there are bags or suitcases in the hotel rooms. He checks the schedule.

This guest is staying in this room for one more night. Where is the guest's bag? Is this the guest's necklace? Or maybe a different guest put it in the tissue box to keep it safe. Maybe that guest forgot about it. This is strange. I will give it to the manager later, he thinks. *Maybe the manager can find the owner.* He puts the necklace in his pocket.

Wei goes to the next room. Soon, he forgets about the necklace.

He is thinking about his test this afternoon. It is a listening test and a writing test. He needs a good score. The test is more important than the necklace. If Wei gets a good score on the test, he can study for one more year. If he gets a bad score on the test, he cannot study at the college next year.

If I don't get a good score, my mother and father will be sad, he thinks. *They worked very hard to get money for me. I have to get a good score on the test.*

Wei finishes cleaning the rooms on the 4th floor. Then, he cleans the dining room. Another worker, Samuel, is helping him. Samuel is older than Wei. He is 30 years old. Wei likes Samuel. They enjoy talking about basketball.

"You look nervous," says Samuel. "Are you OK?"

"I have an important English test this afternoon," says Wei. "If I don't get a good score, I can't study at the college next year."

"Wow, that's important," says Samuel. "But your English is very good. You will get a good score."

"Thank you, Samuel," says Wei.

"If you get a good score, let's have a small party," says Samuel. "There is a new Mexican restaurant near here. Sandra wants to go there. We can go there after work next weekend."

"That's a good idea," says Wei. "Thank you. But maybe I can't go. I don't have much money."

Everyone in this hotel is very kind, thinks Wei. *My job is hard, but I like the people here.*

CHAPTER THREE

At 12:00pm, Wei finishes work. He usually finishes work at 1:00pm, but he asked the manager, "May I finish early today?" The manager said, "Yes, you can finish an hour earlier."

He goes to the staff room. The manager, Samuel and Sandra are in the staff room too. They are talking about the schedule for next week.

"Are you OK, Wei? You look nervous," says the manager. The manager is a man. He is 45 years old. Wei likes him. He is always kind to Wei and the other workers.

"I'm very nervous," says Wei. "I have a test this afternoon."

"Oh really? What kind of test?"

"An English listening and writing test. If I don't get a good score on the test, I can't study at the school next year."

"Oh, that's an important test!" says the manager. "But your English is very good. Don't be nervous!"

"Thank you," says Wei.

Wei takes his work jacket off. When he takes it off, the necklace falls out of his pocket.

"What is that?" asks Sandra. She looks at the necklace. She picks it up.

"It's a diamond necklace! I think this is very expensive!" she says.

The manager, Sandra and Samuel look at Wei.

"Why was this diamond necklace in your pocket, Wei?" asks the manager.

"Oh, I forgot about it. I found it in the tissue box in room four zero one."

The manager thinks it is strange. "Why didn't you give it to me? Why is it in your pocket?"

"I planned to give it to you, but I forgot. I am nervous about my test."

The manager looks at Wei. "Wei, you are a good worker. I want to trust you. But…this is difficult. I'm sorry, but did you plan to take the necklace home?

"What? No, of course not!" says Wei.

"Wei is a good young man. I believe him," says Sandra. "We can trust him."

"I know, but…a guest's necklace was in his pocket. He didn't give me the necklace," says the manager. "This is difficult for me."

"I forgot! Really! I'm very sorry!" says Wei. He looks at the clock. It is 12:15pm He has a test at 3:00pm.

I have to study before my test, he thinks.

"Can we talk about this tomorrow?" he asks the manager.

"No," says the manager. "I am very sorry Wei. But I have to call the police."

"Call the police?" asks Wei. He is very shocked.

"You can't do that!" says Sandra. "Wei forgot about the necklace! He is not a bad man!"

"I know he is not a bad man," says the manager. "But a guest's necklace was in his pocket. He didn't tell me. He didn't give me the necklace. I have to call the police."

"Please don't call the police!" says Wei. "I didn't do a bad thing! Really! I have an important test today. I have to go to college very soon! If the police come, they will talk to me for a long time. I will miss the test!"

"Wei, I understand. But this is a very serious problem," says the manager. "You didn't give me the necklace. It is more important than your test!"

CHAPTER FOUR

The manager goes out of the staff room.

"Sandra, Samuel, what can I do?" asks Wei. "I didn't plan to keep the necklace! Really! I didn't!"

Sandra hugs Wei. "I believe you," she says. "I will tell the police you are a good young man."

"It's OK, Wei. I will tell the police you are a good man, too," says Samuel.

Wei feels very bad. "If the police don't believe me, I will have much trouble," he says. "I will go to jail!"

"You won't go to jail!" says Samuel. "Don't worry! The police will believe you."

"I don't think so," says Wei. "The manager doesn't believe me."

"He does," says Sandra. "But it is difficult for him. The necklace was in your pocket. He has to call the police."

Sandra and Samuel wait with Wei. They eat lunch.

Ten minutes later, the door opens. The manager, a policeman and a policewoman come into the room.

"Come to my office, Wei," says the manager.

"Can I come too?" asks Sandra.

"No, I'm sorry, you can't," says the manager. "Samuel, Sandra, go back to work."

Sandra, Samuel and Wei look at each other.

"You will be OK," says Sandra.

"Thanks," says Wei.

Samuel looks at the police officers. "Wei is a good man," he says.

"Yes, he is a very nice young man," says Sandra.

The police officers don't say anything.

Wei, the manager and the two police officers walk out of the room and go into the manager's office.

"Sit down please," says the manager. The police officers and Wei sit down on three chairs.

"Tell the police officers about the necklace," says the manager.

"I was cleaning room four zero one. I was cleaning the table when I knocked over a glass of water. The water went into the tissue box. I felt something strange in the tissue box. I pulled it out. It was a diamond necklace. I thought, This is strange. I put it in my pocket."

"Why did you put it in your pocket?" asks the policewoman.

"Because I planned to give it to the manager. But I forgot. When I finished work, I took my jacket off, and it fell out of my pocket."

"Did you plan to take the necklace home? Did you plan to sell it?" asks the policeman.

"Of course not!" says Wei.

"But you are a student. Students need money. If you sell the necklace, you can get a lot of money," says the policeman.

"But I am not a bad person!" says Wei. "I need money, so I work hard. I work here at the hotel on Fridays, Saturdays and Sundays."

The policewoman looks at Wei.

"What were you doing yesterday afternoon at four pm?" she asks.

"Yesterday? At four pm? Why?" asks Wei.

"Answer the question," says the policeman.

"I was in my room," says Wei.

"Were you alone?" asks the policewoman.

"Yes, I was alone. I was studying for my test. Why?"

"Because yesterday afternoon, at four pm, someone took a diamond necklace from the jewellery shop near here."

"What?" Wei is shocked.

"We think this is the same necklace," says the policewoman.

"So, do you think I took it from the jewellery shop yesterday?" asks Wei.

"Yes, we think so," says the policeman.

"But I didn't take it! I was studying!" says Wei. He looks at the clock. It is now 1:00pm.

This is very bad. They think I took a necklace from a jewellery shop! And my test starts in two hours! he thinks.

"I didn't take it. Really, I didn't," says Wei. "I found it in the tissue box in room four zero one!"

"Maybe you took the necklace and planned to sell it today, before you go to college," says the policewoman.

"What? Of course not!" says Wei. "Please believe me. Please check the security camera in the shop."

"We checked it. But the person had a mask on his face," says the policewoman.

"I didn't take it!" says Wei.

The policewoman looks at Wei for a long time. Then, she asks the manager, "Who is the guest in room four zero one?"

The manager looks at his computer.

"A man called Jim Saunders," says the manager. The policewoman writes the name in her notebook.

"When did he check in?" she asks.

"Yesterday afternoon," says the manager.

"And when will he check out?" she asks.

"Tomorrow morning," says the manager.

"Is he in his room now?" asks the policewoman.

"I don't know. I will ask a staff member to check," says the manager. He picks up the phone and calls the front desk.

"Please send a staff member to room four zero one," he says. "I want to talk to Mr Saunders." He puts the phone down.

A few minutes later, the phone rings.

"Hello?" says the manager. "OK, thank you."

He puts the phone down.

"Mr Saunders is not in his room," he says.

"We will take Wei to the police station," says the policewoman. "If Mr Saunders comes back, please call us."

"OK, I will call you," says the manager.

Wei is shocked. "No! I can't go to the police station!" he says. "I have a test at three o'clock!"

"This necklace is more important than your test!" says the policeman.

CHAPTER FIVE

Bert Johnson walks to his hotel. He stops. There is a police car.

Oh no, he thinks. *The police! Did someone find the necklace? I can't go back to the hotel.*

He sees a policewoman and a policeman. They are walking out of the hotel. There is a young man with them. The young man looks sad and angry. Bert goes into a shop. He watches the police officers and the young man from the shop window.

Who is that man? Why is he with the police officers? Did something bad happen in the hotel?

The police officers and the young man get into the police car. They drive away.

I have to check the necklace, thinks Bert. *I have to go back to my hotel room, but maybe it is a little dangerous now.*

Bert walks out of the shop and walks to another street. There is a small café. He goes into the café and orders a cup of coffee and a sandwich.

I will wait here for an hour, he thinks.

CHAPTER SIX

Wei and the police officers walk into the police station. Wei is very sad and angry. They walk into a room. The room has a table and four chairs. There is a TV screen on the table.

"Sit down," says the policeman.

Wei sits down. The policeman switches on the TV. Wei watches a video from a security camera. It is from a security camera in the jewellery shop.

"Look at this man here," says the policewoman.

Wei watches the man on the screen. The man is wearing a mask. He hits a glass case with a hammer. Then, he takes a necklace and runs out of the shop.

"Is that you?" asks the policeman.

"No! Of course not!" says Wei. "That is not me!" Wei is angry. He stands up. "I came to America to study English. I like America. I want to study here next year too. I want to study hard and get a good job. My mother and father worked very hard to get money. I study hard for my parents and my future!"

"Sit down!" says the policeman. "The man in the shop is tall. You are tall. He is thin. You are thin. I think you are the man in the shop."

"It is not me!" says Wei. "It is not me! Yesterday, I was studying in my room for my test. Please! I have a test today! I have to go to college now!"

"You can't go to college. We think you took the necklace," says the policewoman.

"Show me the video again," says Wei.

The policewoman starts the video again.

The man walks into the shop. He breaks the glass case. "Stop the video!" says Wei.

The policewoman stops the video.

"Look! Look at the man's hand! He has a small tattoo on his hand! I don't have a tattoo!" says Wei.

The policeman and the policewoman look at the screen very carefully.

"I know that tattoo!" says the policewoman. "That man is Bert Johnson!"

"Bert Johnson?" asks the policeman.

"Yes," says the policewoman.

"Who is Bert Johnson?" asks Wei.

"This man on the screen is Bert Johnson. We know him very well. He is from Boston. He took a ring from a jewellery shop in New York last year. He was in jail for six months. Two years ago, he took a necklace and a bracelet from a jewellery shop in Boston," says the policewoman. "He was in jail for six months then, too."

"Do you believe me now?" asks Wei.

"We have to talk to this man," says the policewoman.

"What time is it?" asks Wei.

The policewoman looks at her watch. "It is two fifty," she says.

"Oh no! My test!!" says Wei.

"I'm sorry, but this is more important. The necklace is fifty thousand dollars," says the policeman.

"My test is important to me," says Wei.

Then, another policeman walks into the room.

"The manager of the hotel called. Jim Saunders came back to his hotel room," says the policeman.

"I will go to the hotel," says the policewoman.

"Can I go to college now?" asks Wei.

"No, you have to stay here," says the policeman.

I can't take my test. I can't study at the college next year. I have to go back to China. My mother and father will be very sad and angry, thinks Wei. *What am I going to do?*

CHAPTER SEVEN

Bert Johnson is in room 401. He is looking under the bed.

Where is the necklace? he thinks. *I put it in the tissue box, but now, there is a new tissue box! Why?* He looks in the bathroom. He cannot find the necklace.

Then, there is a knock on the door.

"Mr Saunders? This is the manager. Can you open the door please?"

Bert is shocked. He doesn't want to open the door.

"I'm busy," he says. "Can you come back later?"

"Bert Johnson! This is the police! Open the door!" says the policewoman.

Oh no! thinks Bert. *How did the police find me?*

Very slowly, he opens the door.

The policewoman and the manager walk into the room. The policewoman looks at Bert's hand. There is a tattoo on his hand.

"How did you find me?" asks Bert.

"It was very easy," says the policewoman. "In the shop yesterday, you covered your face. But you didn't cover your tattoo!"

"How did you find the necklace?" asks Bert.

"The cleaner knocked over a glass of water. The tissues were wet. He found the necklace in there," says the manager.

"You are coming to the police station with me!" says the policewoman. She holds Bert's arm and takes him out of the room and into the elevator.

The manager is angry. "You took the necklace and put it in a room in my hotel. Now, one of my staff members has trouble because of you! He had an important test today, but he is in the police station. He can't take the test!"

"I will try to help Wei," says the policewoman. "I don't know if I can help him, but I will try."

CHAPTER EIGHT

The policewoman takes Wei to college. It is 4:30pm. The test has finished. They go into the school. Wei sees some of his friends.

"Wei!" says Jose. "What happened? Why didn't you come to the test? Why are you with the police?"

"I will tell you later," says Wei.

Wei and the policewoman walk to the college head teacher's office. The policewoman knocks on the door. "It's the police!" says the policewoman.

The head teacher opens the door. He is very shocked.

"What happened?" he asks.

"Can we come in?" asks the policewoman.

"Of course," says the head teacher. "Please, sit down."

"Yesterday, a man took a diamond necklace from a jewellery store in the city," says the policewoman. "He put it in a tissue box in his hotel room. Wei has a part-time job in the hotel. He was cleaning the room, and he found the necklace. We thought, *Wei took the necklace.* So, we took him to the police station. But we made a mistake. Wei didn't take the necklace."

"I see," says the head teacher.

"But there is a problem," says the policewoman. "Wei had an important test this afternoon."

"Yes, he did," says the head teacher.

"But he couldn't take the test. So, can he take the test now?"

"Please!" says Wei.

"Wei helped us to catch a bad man," says the policewoman. The man often takes jewellery from shops. Wei is a hero. Please help him."

"A hero? We have a hero in our college? That is great," says the head teacher. "Well done, Wei. You can take the test now."

"Oh, thank you!" says Wei.

"Thank you," says the policewoman. She looks at Wei. "Good luck!" she says.

The head teacher takes Wei to a classroom. He gives Wei the test paper. Wei does the test. It is a two-hour test and Wei feels very tired, but it is easy for him.

I used English a lot today, he thinks. *That was good practice for me!*

Later, he goes to a café with his friends. He tells them the story about the necklace and the police. His friends are very surprised.

"Now you have a good story to tell people about your time in New York!" says Jose.

"Yes, I have a good story," says Wei. "If I pass my test, the story will have a happy ending!"

CHAPTER NINE

A week later, Wei gets his score for his test. He passed! He got 90%. He is very happy. He goes to work on Saturday. He is in the staff room with Sandra and Samuel. They are eating lunch.

"How was your test?" asks Sandra.

"It was good. I got ninety percent," says Wei.

"Congratulations!" says Sandra.

Then, the manager walks into the room.

"Wei, I want to talk to you. Please come to my office," he says.

Wei, Sandra and Samuel look at each other.

Why does he want to talk to me? thinks Wei. He goes out of the room and walks to the manager's office.

There is a woman in the office. She smiles at Wei.

"Hello Wei. I am Vicky from the jewellery store," she says.

"Hello. Nice to meet you," says Wei.

"You helped us last week," says Vicky. "You found the necklace. So, I want to give you something."

Vicky gives Wei an envelope.

"What's this?" asks Wei.

"Five thousand dollars," says Vicky.

"What? Five thousand dollars? But, why?"

"The necklace is fifty thousand dollars. It is very expensive. We want to say thank you. So please, take the money."

Wei cannot believe it.

"You are a good worker Wei. I believed you, but I had to call the police. You had trouble at college. I'm sorry," says the manager. "So

I will give you a bonus of a thousand dollars."

"Really?" Wei smiles at Vicky and the manager. "Thank you! Thank you so much!" he says.

I have a lot of money now, he thinks. *I can quit my job. But, I enjoy working here. I can practice English. And I like my co-workers. They believed me. They helped me a lot. I want to say thank you to them. I have an idea...*

CHAPTER TEN

It is the next weekend. Wei, Samuel, Sandra and some other workers are sitting in the new Mexican restaurant. Wei asked everyone to come to the restaurant. He is going to pay for everyone's dinner and drinks.

"Congratulations Wei!" says everyone. "And thank you for tonight!"

"Thank you," says Wei. "You all believed me. You trusted me. You are my friends. The day of my test was a bad day, but I got a good score. I can study at the college next year."

"I'm so happy," says Sandra. "I enjoy working with you. We all enjoy working with you. But yes, it was a bad day."

"Let's not talk about the bad day," says Samuel. "Let's forget about that. Let's talk about something happy. Let's talk about basketball!"

"Basketball? That's not interesting," says Sandra.

"Yes, it is," says Samuel.

"Let's talk about movies!" says Karen, another worker.

"No, let's talk about summer vacations!" says Linda from the hotel restaurant.

Wei laughs. "I got a good score because you all talk about many different things. It is good English practice for me. Thank you!"

THANK YOU

Thank you for reading Wei's Part-Time Job. We hope you enjoyed Wei's story. (Word count: 4,375)

There are quizzes about this book on our free study site I Talk You Talk Press EXTRA. http://italk-youtalk.com

If you would like to read more graded readers, please visit our website http://www.italkyoutalk.com

Other Level 1 graded readers include
A Business Trip to New York
A Homestay in Auckland
A Trip to London
Dear Ellen
Emily's Bag
Haruna's Story Part 1
Haruna's Story Part 2
Haruna's Story Part 3
Ken's Story Part 1
Ken's Story Part 2
Life is Surprising!
Strange Stories
The Christmas Present
The Old Hospital
We Met Online

ABOUT THE AUTHOR

I Talk You Talk Press is a Japan-based publisher of language textbooks, graded readers and language learning/teaching resources.

Our team is made up of highly experienced language teachers and translators, who have all studied at least one additional language to an advanced level.

This experience enables us to design our materials from the perspective of both the teacher and the learner. We consult with both teachers and language learners when designing our textbooks and graded readers, and test our materials extensively in the classroom before publication.

We are a fast-growing press, and currently publish graded readers for learners of English. We publish new graded readers monthly.

www.ingramcontent.com/pod-product-compliance
Lightning Source LLC
LaVergne TN
LVHW051518170726
843492LV00002B/991